IMAGES
of America

PRICKETTS FORT

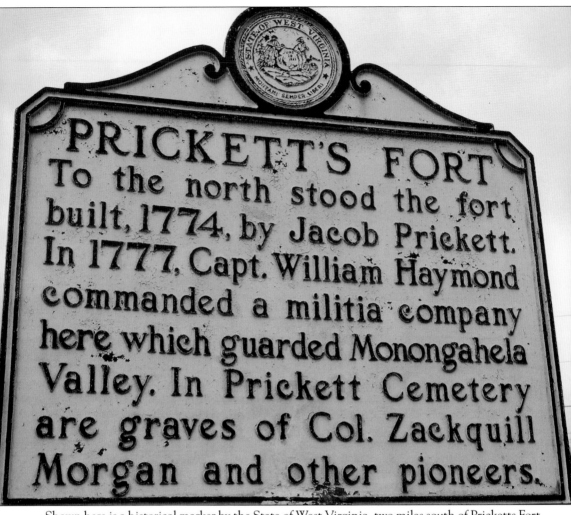

Shown here is a historical marker by the State of West Virginia, two miles south of Pricketts Fort State Park. It reads: "Pricketts Fort To the north stood the fort built, 1774, by Jacob Prickett. In 1777, Capt. William Haymond commanded a militia company here, which guarded Monongahela Valley. In Prickett Cemetery are graves of Col. Zackquill Morgan and other pioneers." (Courtesy of the Pricketts Fort Memorial Foundation.)

ON THE COVER: Built on the land of Jacob Prickett in 1774, the original fort was used to protect the area settlers from raiding parties of Native Americans. Today, the historic fort and 19th-century Job Prickett House can be seen by adults and children alike. It is for those who have an appreciation of the past or want to experience a journey by which their ancestors walked and lived. The fort is used as an education facility to teach visitors about the past and how the way of life in the backwoods of the western Virginia frontier would have been in the 18th and 19th centuries. (Courtesy of the Pricketts Fort Memorial Foundation.)

IMAGES
of America

PRICKETTS FORT

Greg Bray

ARCADIA
PUBLISHING

Published by Arcadia Publishing
Charleston, South Carolina

Printed in the United States of America

Library of Congress Control Number: 2013951263

For all general information, please contact Arcadia Publishing:
Telephone 843-853-2070
Fax 843-853-0044
E-mail sales@arcadiapublishing.com
For customer service and orders:
Toll-Free 1-888-313-2665

Visit us on the Internet at www.arcadiapublishing.com

*This book is dedicated to all of the people who traveled westward
over the mountains to settle this untamed wilderness and to
those who sacrificed their lives for our independence.*

CONTENTS

ACKNOWLEDGMENTS

An endeavor of this nature never falls entirely on one person's shoulders. Though his or her name will be seen on the front cover and some may lecture and attend book signings, the authoring of a book is accomplished with a team effort. The bulk of this is done by a dedicated staff who makes the phone calls, does the legwork, and who feels as strongly about a project as the author who receives the recognition. This book is no different.

There are many dedicated and energetic people who tirelessly helped with this book. First and foremost, I would like to thank my assistant director Alisha Lilly, who helped with the organization and typing and kept me on track to meet my deadlines, and to my administrative assistant Monika Koon, who helped proofread and grammar-check my work. My thanks also goes to Andrew Knez, a historic artist from Pennsylvania who gave me permission to use as many of his historic paintings and prints that I needed. I also want to thank editors Lissie Cain and Julia Simpson at Arcadia Publishing for making this book come to be.

A special thank-you goes to all of the members and donors of the Pricketts Fort Memorial Foundation. Pricketts Fort would not exist without you.

So, once again, I would like to thank these people; without them, this book would have been a monumental undertaking and one that would have, I am sure, fallen short of its intended mark.

Unless otherwise noted, all images in this collection appear courtesy of the Pricketts Fort Memorial Foundation.

INTRODUCTION

Pricketts Fort was originally built in 1774 on the land of Jacob Prickett, during what is known as Lord Dunmore's War. Built on a small rise near the confluence of Pricketts Creek and the Monongahela River by local militia, Pricketts Fort provided refuge for approximately 80 families. The fort itself was large by 18th-century standards. The fort had blockhouses at each corner with walls 12 feet high and 110 feet in length. Although the fort was never attacked, many outlying homes were and many settlers lost their lives.

Nothing is known of the demise of Pricketts Fort, except that tradition indicates between 1789 and 1799, the fort fell into disrepair and had discontinued to be in use by area settlers.

The first efforts to rebuild Pricketts Fort began in 1927, when a commission of three men was appointed by the governor of West Virginia to buy no more than 10 acres of land in the area of Fairmont, which was to include the site of the original fort, when funds became available. These lands were in the process of being purchased from the Prickett family, but the Great Depression prevented any such land acquisitions to be completed.

After World War II, new members were appointed to this commission every few years, but the land was not purchased until 1966 when the US Army Corps of Engineers obtained the property. Fortunately, at that time, the Marion County Historical Society intervened to prevent the current site of Pricketts Fort from becoming a parking lot. The West Virginia's Department of Natural Resources had leased the land for the further development of a state park and recreational facility. Then the Department of Natural Resources and the Marion County Historical Society helped in the formation of the Pricketts Fort Memorial Foundation.

In 1970, the foundation was incorporated as a nonprofit organization dedicated to the preservation and interpretation of the history and culture of the Upper Monongahela Valley. The foundation's first act of business was facilitating memberships and to secure funds to rebuild Pricketts Fort. At the same time, the Marion County Historical Society was given the task of researching 18th-century construction methods and having working drawings prepared from which the fort structure could be built, which resulted in three years of research. This involved visiting other forts and cabins in the region. The final drawings from which the fort would be modeled after were not finished until after July 1974. Early in the planning stages, it was decided by the foundation and the construction committee that the fort should be constructed out of salvaged logs from houses and barns, which were still quite plentiful in the 1970s. Newspaper articles told of the plans to build Pricketts Fort and the donations of log buildings came in faster than the foundation could procure the funds to have them brought to the construction site. In August 1973, with $4,000 in the bank and small loans from three different area banks, the foundation was far from the estimated $150,000 needed to complete the project of rebuilding Pricketts Fort.

By the time the winter of 1973 hit, the foundation's money had dried up, but cash donations and memberships continued to come in throughout the winter. It also became apparent that at the rate donations were coming in, the foundation would not meet its target day of May 30, 1976, for opening. The foundation then decided to ask for financial assistant from the State of West Virginia. They entered into negotiations with then governor Arch A. Moore Jr. who showed some interest in the project. Upon being shown pictures of the progress of construction and being impressed with how much work was completed with little financial resources, Governor Moore and the state legislature appropriated $200,000 to complete the project.

Work commenced in October 1974 and continued throughout the winter when weather would permit. By the spring of 1975, the project began to take shape. By early spring of 1976, the realization set in that the completion date of May 30 would come and go. A new date of June 30, 1976, was set, and the fort was turned over to the foundation on July 3, just in time for the bicentennial.

Pricketts Fort was brought about by a cooperating effort in preservation of culture and history. The land, which belongs to the US Army Corps of Engineers, is leased to the West Virginia Department of Natural Resources. The Pricketts Fort Memorial Foundation then became a vendor, through a concession agreement with the Department of Natural Resources.

Every effort was made to keep an accurate record of buildings donated and by whom. This was accomplished for the most part, and the foundation does have a donors list that is too lengthy for this publication. Out of the 41 donated log structures, which provided 14,000 linear feet of timbers, 11,000 feet were used. Ninety percent of all the logs used were of white oak with the remainder being other types of oak and American chestnut.

Over the past 37 years, thousands of antiques have been donated for the interpretive programs at Pricketts Fort. As well as hundreds of thousands of dollars in memberships and donations for other building projects in the park, like the 19th-century Job Prickett House, the new Bray Blacksmith Shop, a new visitor center, and most recently a newly refurbished outdoor amphitheater. So in reality, the original fort was built by cooperative and community efforts in 1774 and was rebuilt by the same efforts in 1976 and still continues 37 years later.

Over the years, many books and small publications have been written about Pricketts Fort and its history. What has not been written about is how Pricketts Fort became a state park, the vision of what some people thought the park should be, and its continued growth over the last 37 years. Very few records exist about the people and happenings of the original Pricketts Fort. For the reconstructed fort and state park, a lot is known but is discussed very little. As the author, I find this history to be just as important as the history of the original fort. Many of the photographs that have been used in this book have never been seen by the public. Others, like the images of the US Army Corps of Engineers, have been stuck in a file cabinet since the early 1970s. As the author, I hope this book is neither boring nor self-indulgent.

One

THE EARLY HISTORY
OF PRICKETTS FORT

Glenn D. Lough's *Now and Long Ago: A History of the Marion County Area* includes the following quote from early trader Charles Polk: "When first I came to the Monongahela there were panthers, buffalo, wolves, elk, beaver, deer, and bears. The Indians from the lower Allegheny and upper Ohio rivers were constantly in the woods hunting, trapping, and trading skins with the white traders at their hunting camps and meeting places. The traders took their skins from here to Shannopin's Town and from there by packhorse to Philadelphia and later to Crogans Post and still later to Winchester, VA. On the west side of the Monongahela, just above the mouth of Paw Paw Creek was a popular place of rendezvous where white traders and Indians met, frolicked, and did their trading. This place was particularly favored by the Indians for the fine paw paws that grew in abundance there."

Charles Polk traded in the area in the 1740s and 1750s, about 30 years before Pricketts Fort would be built in 1774. It is reputed that Polk gave Jacob Prickett, David Morgan, John Snodgrass, and Pharoah Ryley directions on how to find the Monongahela River and its tributaries. These men would all be part of the Prickett settlement several years later. By the time Pricketts Fort was built, Charles Polk was living in the Ohio country.

This is the Monongahela River very near Paw Paw Creek. The creek is about a mile northwest of where Pricketts Fort would later stand. This area today is still sparsely populated with plenty of forest and wildlife. Charles Polk traded in this area in the 1740s, well before any settlement. It would be 30 more years before Pricketts Fort would be built in 1774.

Seated are two former employees of Pricketts Fort, William Sembello and Andrew Chidester, who are portraying American Indians in a trading camp much like the one that would have been seen during the time of Charles Polk.

Lough's *Now and Long Ago* also includes the following quote from Keziah Batlen Shearer (1776–1872): "The living in old times was hard. Women and children cried a great deal and the men and boys cussed a lot and everybody prayed enough in church, in the fields, in the woods, wherever and whenever they had a feeling for it. But mostly we all just laughed about nothing much to eat, I mean and the Indians sneaking around. Poor half naked fellows. And we abided, and it was wonderful. Seems people don't have enough good work to do these days. If they did have, and did it, they'd feel much better about everything. Hard working men and women are hard-loving, too. And that's what it takes to make the mare go hardworking and hardloving. We were lonesome a lot. Everybody was lonesome, I guess, in the old times. The woods caused it. The woods were gloomy, but of mornings and evenings they were kind of grand, too. We put up with a lot of trouble, but we stayed brave, and God was by us every minute, you know."

After the French and Indian War, the Treaty of 1763 (or the Treaty of Paris) was signed. This treaty designated all of the land west of the Appalachian Mountains as lands for Native Americans and forbade all settlements by colonists west of the mountains, which was typically the hunting grounds for a lot of the eastern tribes. These lands provided food, shelter, and furs, the latter of which was the basis of their economy, trading with the white traders. This painting by Andrew Knez, *Cherokee Hunters*, depicts the quintessential Native American traversing the Appalachian region, providing for himself and his family.

A *New Beginning* by Andrew Knez, in this author's opinion, depicts the migration of settlers crossing the Allegheny Mountains to the fertile Monongahela Valley. Although the colonists were under orders from British rule not to settle west of the Appalachian Mountains, there was a steady migration of settlers. Colonists were beckoned by the cheap fertile land of the Ohio Valley, where the settlers could live by their own laws and avoid British Rule.

There were several factors that went into the orders for forts to be built in the Monongahela Valley, from random killings of pacifist American Indians to the murder of Chief Logan's family. Chief Logan, who was a peaceful chief from the Mingo tribe, was not present when his family was murdered but swore revenge upon all settlers after this occurred. This is a photograph of Aaron Bosnick, a former interpreter of Pricketts Fort, portraying a Native American.

Not only were Chief Logan and the Mingos troublesome, but other threats to the settlers in the Monongahela Valley came from the Shawnee, Delaware, Wyondot, and Cherokee. This is a photograph of an unidentified reenactor at Pricketts Fort.

Through the orders of Gov. Lord Dunmore, a defensive line of forts in the Monongahela Valley were to be built; one of these forts would be Pricketts Fort. From the fall of 1774 to the spring of 1775 Pricketts Fort was erected. This is a photograph of Pricketts Fort during the winter of 1976.

Stephen Morgan, who was 12 years old when Pricketts Fort was built, said that the fort was 110 square feet with four corner blockhouses and 16 small cabins with roofs sloping inwards and two large cabins in the center of the fort. An outer stockade of fence 150-yards square, used to secure livestock, was also built, which would have made Pricketts Fort one of the largest forts in the Monongahela Valley. This is a photograph of some of the small cabins inside the fort and one of the four blockhouses.

Several native interpreters prepare for war—note the painted faces and tattoos. Also, some of the spoils of war are visible with one native wearing a red colonial waistcoat, today known as a vest. From left to right, are Bill Graham, Aaron Bosnick, Jon Miller, unidentified, and John Brasuk. All of these people have volunteered at Pricketts Fort.

Native interpreter Aaron Bosnick discusses his native clothing and accoutrements with the day's visitors. Aaron Bosnick represents a Shawnee warrior, as one would have looked during the latter half of the 18th century. The Shawnee used what is now West Virginia as a hunting ground, which was essential to their survival and the economic well-being of their tribe.

As soon as tensions between the settlers and natives came to a head in 1774, militias were formed and Pricketts Fort was built. The fort was built by the local inhabitants, who also formed the first militia. Boys as young as 16 and men as old as 60 were required to be in a militia. This photograph, which was taken soon after the fort was reconstructed in 1976, shows some unidentified reenactors marching to muster.

In the early days of the original fort, as many as 200–250 men, women, and children would have occupied the fort and its surrounding grounds. As time went on, these numbers would have dwindled as more forts were built. These numbers are based on known families living in a five-mile radius of Pricketts Fort, with an average of four to five children.

One of the requirements of the members of the militia, just like today's National Guard, was to complete drills once a month. There were at least four different militia units known to be stationed at Pricketts Fort during the 1770s–1780s. One of these units was here during the winter, which was very unusual. This photograph is of unidentified reenactors at Pricketts Fort who are standing in drill formation getting ready to do their daily drills.

In times of danger, families brought almost everything they thought was of value with them to the fort, including their livestock—if that family had the opportunity to do so. The reason for this was they never knew how long they would have to stay, and if there was a raid on their farm, their cabin would most likely be burnt. This is a photograph of a frontier family's personal belongings.

A view of the interior of one of the small cabins inside of the fort depicts its use by a local settler in times of trouble from Native Americans. This was known as "forting up," and it was described as something simply tolerated by the early settlers.

A view of the original road leading to the fort from the south is seen here. This road was used for generations by Jacob Pickett's descendants and people of the community. Remnants of this road are still visible today and part of it is used as a nature trail.

Often animals were housed inside forts. Animals were brought in with the fort's inhabitants to keep them from being harmed by Native Americans during raids. Most forts had some kind of fence or stock pen to contain the animals during times of trouble. Other forts during times of trouble let the livestock roam about inside the walls. This often caused great excitement if the fort was attacked and caused a lot of confusion between the defenders of the fort and the animals. Today at Pricketts Fort, these are some of the animals a visitor can see on a day-to-day basis.

Charity Taylor Prickett was the daughter-in-law to Jacob Prickett Sr. She was married to Josiah Prickett, and later she was known to everyone as "Aunt Charity." This photograph is of a stoneware crock, which was owned by Charity Taylor Prickett.

This photograph of an original packsaddle was used by settlers and traders like Charles Polk to transport household items as well as furs. These handmade wooden saddles were necessary to transport goods over the mountains and along trade routes as well as to the fort in times of trouble.

This photograph is of an original document box owned by Nathaniel Cochran. He was an early settler who lived within seven miles of Pricketts Fort. Cochran was captured by Native Americans and imprisoned by the British for five years.

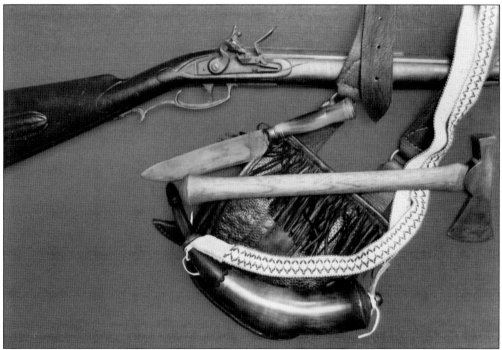

This photograph shows some of the necessary tools used by the early settlers. A rifle, which was very expensive, took about a year's wages for the average settler. Pictured here is a knife and tomahawk (both blacksmith made), a powder horn, and a hunting bag. The hunting bag was used to carry gun tools, a spare flint, and the like.

This would have been a typical scene inside the fort of men talking of the upcoming campaign or with war. This scene would have played over and over again at Pricketts Fort during the 18th century as militias would have been formed for different campaigns against the Native Americans in the Ohio Valley or while men were being recruited to scout the trails used by the Shawnee who came from the Ohio Valley to the Monongahela River Valley to conduct their raids on the area settlers.

Two reenactors converse at a small hut. Huts like this would have been a common scene around the fort during times of trouble. Due to the large number of people who used the fort, men, boys, and sometimes whole families would have to stay just outside of the fort walls.

In the winter, forts were used very little in the Monongahela Valley. Native Americans would not have traveled from the Ohio country where their villages were—unless there was some kind of extended warm weather (known as an Indian summer). Both photographs depict the quietness and peacefulness winter brought at Pricketts Fort. Today, an Indian summer is known as a warm up after a hard freeze or frost. At the time of the original fort, an Indian summer meant a chance for a quick Indian raid on the community.

Pricketts Creek, which was named after Jacob Prickett, is a meandering stream about four to five miles long, which empties into the Monongahela River just past the site of the fort. Today, a visitor to the park will travel about two miles of the creek before reaching the park. This photograph demonstrates the beautiful scenery of Pricketts Creek coming into Pricketts Fort State Park.

Harvest season at the time of the original fort would have been a busy and exciting time of the year. Families would have taken to the woods to gather nuts and whatever fruits were available. Crops were harvested, which was crucial for the winter months, but most importantly, incursions from Native Americans would have been less likely to occur. This photograph of corn and other crops, like beans and squash (known as the "Three Sisters" by Native Americans), are grown at Pricketts Fort as part of the daily interpretive program.

Stoneware is a product made from area clay and fired in an oven to make them more durable. These were common storage vessels in the 18th century. This type of vessel, fired or, in some cases, unfired, has been used by man for millennia. Shown here is a photograph of a group of stoneware crocks and bowls, made by a potter at Pricketts Fort.

This scene was probably played over and over at the time of the original fort; American Indians looking out wondering what was to become of their future and their children's futures, much the way many do today. This photograph of two Native American reenactors sitting on the bank of Pricketts Creek was taken during the Fall Festival at Pricketts Fort.

Two

THE CHANGING
LANDSCAPE AND THE
CORPS OF ENGINEERS

After World War II, the US Army Corps of Engineers started developing a lock and dam system in the Pittsburgh district to help control flooding in the Ohio Valley region. As a result, several manmade lakes and other features were created, giving birth to several state parks where boating and other water recreations were developed. In 1956, the US Army Corps of Engineers secured the site of what is now Prickett's Fort State Park, and, in turn, the corps leased 188 acres to the West Virginia Department of Natural Resources for development into a state park, which was to include parking, river access, and restrooms. In 1966, work on this aspect of the park began, which set into motion the negotiations by the Marion County Historical Society, the Department of Natural Resources, and the US Army Corps of Engineers to secure the land for Pricketts Fort to be built.

This chapter will focus on the development of the state park's infrastructure on how it was developed, why it was important to community, and further development of the park itself.

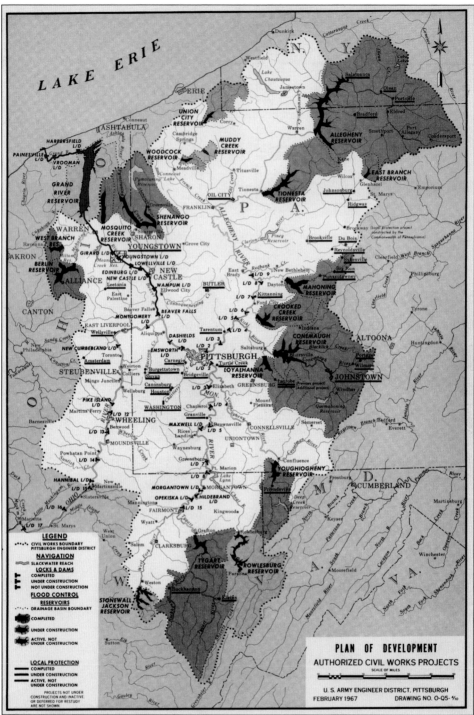

A 1967 map shows the plans of development from north central West Virginia north to Lake Erie by the US Army Corps of Engineers, west to Marietta, Ohio, and east to Johnstown, Pennsylvania. This plan encompassed hundreds of miles of river and about 20 reservoirs and created more navigable river miles. (Courtesy of US Army Corps of Engineers.)

This photograph was taken of the Opekiska Lock and Dam as a tugboat passes through pushing a barge. Built by the US Army Corps of Engineers, this put Prickett's Fort State Park, well on its way to becoming a recreational area as well as Marion County's leading tourist attraction, on the map.

At the time of this writing, the lock system on the Monongahela River has been interrupted by lack of water traffic, creating a government shutdown of the locks. Today, the locks are basically shutdown to boat traffic except by appointment only. The photograph shows the massive gate being operated at Opekiska Lock and Dam.

This is an early view of the entrance to where Pricketts Fort would later be built. This is a sign pointing to where the original fort once stood. Note both of the narrow, unpaved roads. The left fork is the Montana Mine Road, and the right fork was originally a railroad service road from the 1920s, which was later used by the Prickett family to access their property. In 1967, this road became the entrance road for the state park.

This view shows the paved entrance and the widened Montana Mine Road. This view is of the same intersection as seen on the previous page. The Montana Mine Road has been visibly widened and paving has begun on the park's entrance road. Many roads in rural West Virginia in the 1960s and early 1970s were still unimproved and unpaved. This is what kept West Virginia behind in many ways, but also added a certain charm to exploring the Appalachian region for tourists from more metropolitan areas.

A 1966 photograph shows an early view of a 90-car parking lot. The house on the right has yet to be torn down. Today, that space is a picnic area, and beyond the railroad trestle is part of the rail-trail system of West Virginia. At the end of this excavation work was a new boat ramp. (Courtesy of US Army Corps of Engineers.)

This 1967 photograph shows a paved parking area for cars and boats. Note the boat-launching ramp to the right of the pavement roller. What a difference a year makes! This photograph was taken halfway up the hill from where the fort now stands. What a commanding view this would have made to the early settlers. (Courtesy of US Army Corps of Engineers.)

From the sign of Pricketts Fort on page 33, the road continued past one of the earliest cemeteries in Marion County. The cemetery (enclosed by the white fence on the left) dates to the time of the original fort. For many of the fort's inhabitants, this was their final resting place—the same is true for their descendants in the 19th and 20th centuries. (Courtesy of US Army Corps of Engineers.)

This photograph is a continuation of the entrance road to the parking lot and boat-launching area. On the right-hand side of the photograph one can see a construction trailer—this is about where the reconstructed fort stands today. (Courtesy of US Army Corps of Engineers.)

Shown here are views of the boat-launching area under construction. The area had not been flooded by the lock at Opekiska yet at the time of the above photograph (March 1967). This would be the first of two boat ramps; the second would be built 30 years later. The water that is seen in the photograph is Pricketts Creek. This photograph below of the same boat ramp was taken four months after the first photograph and shows the flooded area, which is now called Prickett's Creek Bay. Just like today, no creek channel can be seen. (Courtesy of US Army Corps of Engineers.)

Before being flooded by the Opekiska lock, people could clearly see the lay of the land and Pricketts Creek's main channel, much like one would have seen at the time of the original fort. Also note the flat bottom land along the creek, which was farmland during the 19th century.

This photograph shows the state park and the Montana Mine Road drainage system being installed. Most of this area today is a natural sanctuary for wildlife. The home in the upper right of the photograph is the park superintendent's home.

This pre-construction photograph was taken before any excavation work. The view is looking from the parking area. Until this time, the lay of the land had changed very little from the time of the original fort—only the railroad bed, in the upper third of the photograph, had changed the landscape to any degree. (Courtesy of US Army Corps of Engineers).

The Opekiska Lock and Dam is visible here. The stream on the right is White Day Creek, which empties into the Monongahela River. Many hair-raising adventures took place in this area at the time of the original fort. This is about five miles north of Pricketts Fort.

This photograph shows the Hoult Lock and Dam, part of the early flood-control dam system on the Monongahela River. It was eventually discontinued, along with the one at Opekiska, which was replaced with a new lock in the early 1960s.

Three

THE RECONSTRUCTION OF PRICKETTS FORT

The fort's reconstruction period is the most important aspect of Prickett's Fort State Park, in the author's opinion. Without the historical fort, the story of the Pricketts and the other families that made up the Prickett community would be left untold. Without the determination of a few family members like Irene Prickett and the Marion County Historical Society, this chapter and the proceeding chapters would have to be left untold.

The reconstruction of Pricketts Fort actually began in 1971 when a concession agreement with the West Virginia Department of Natural Resources and the Pricketts Fort Memorial Foundation was forged. In 1972, concept drawings were prepared and submitted to the Department of Natural Resources and US Army Corps of Engineers. In 1973, construction commenced in August, and the first blockhouse was built. By the spring of 1975, two blockhouses, two cabins, and what is now known as the meetinghouse were completed, and the fort opened with limited activities and with volunteer interpreters. On June 29, 1976, the park opened its historic attractions to the public with a grand ceremony and the 249th Army Band, the Virginia Militia Color Guard, and a host of distinguished guests from the Department of Natural Resources.

This is the first blockhouse and wall section to be put into place during the reconstruction. The north corner, visible here, is believed to be made out of the oldest logs donated to the project. Some of the logs date back to the original fort. These logs came from the Pitcher or Calder Haymond cabin, which was about a mile from the fort.

This is the outer view of the north corner. This section was the first part that was completed in 1974, and it was that first section that was shown to Gov. Arch M. Moore, which prompted the State of West Virginia to secure the funds to finance the project.

This photograph is of a monument erected in 1916 by the Sons of the American Revolution and marks the site of Pricketts Fort, which was built on the land of Jacob Prickett in 1774. The Society of the Sons of the American Revolution is an institution that perpetuates the memory of the men who, in the military, naval, and civil service of the colonies and of the Continental Congress, by their acts or counsel, achieved the independence of the country and of prominent events connected with the revolution; to collect and secure for preservation, the rolls, records and other documents relating to that period. It was built to inspire the members of the society with the patriotic spirit of their forefathers, and it marks the site of Pricketts Fort.

This is the original placement of the monument, marking the site of the original fort. It was moved by the US Army Corps of Engineers in late 1966 or early 1967 so work could continue on the state park facility. The monument in the center of the upper third of the photograph is clearly visible.

The same part of the construction is shown here as on page 42, except a partial chimney has been added. Furthermore, the east wall has just been started. Note that the fire box and chimney is made out of wood. This is called waddle and daub construction. It was very common in the 18th century. This was also very easy to catch fire if one was not careful.

By late 1975, a lot of progress had been made. All four blockhouses had been completed and the two main buildings had been erected. Note the jib pole, the triangle-shaped rig on the right side of the photograph. This was to help lift the heavy timbers.

This view shows the heavy timbers used in the reconstruction of Pricketts Fort. Almost all of the timbers were donated by area families from original log cabins and barns. A lot of these families are descendants of the same families who built the original Pricketts Fort. Most of the timbers used were white oak.

Shingles made from white oak timber were used on the roofs during reconstruction, and they were typically made during the winter months when there was time for such work. This work could be done inside or out of the weather. In the very early construction of cabins, bark was often used until the necessary tools could be acquired to make oak shingles.

Photographed here is a chimney of stone, wood, and clay, also known as waddle and daub. This type of construction was typical in the 18th century but was susceptible to catching fire. Many towns required its inhabitants to build chimneys of brick or stone to help combat this problem.

This is one of the fort's four blockhouses. Blockhouses were used as a lookout for a fort and were also the last defensive position that could be used if the walls were ever breached by the enemy. The chinking, as it is called, is the filler between the logs, which has been finished, and only the door needs to be installed.

Pictured is a view of the second of the largest structures within the fort. Today, this building houses the Prickett Trading Post and Gunshop. Note the large pile of stone to be used in making the large fireplace and chimney. Tons of stone was donated to be used in the fort's reconstruction.

A group looks on as work progresses on the reconstruction process. Note the completion of the dry laid chimney on building number one, today known as the meetinghouse. Dry laid is a technique where stone is stacked or laid without the use of mortar, which is much more difficult and time consuming.

This view of the construction looks towards the south with still only one blockhouse completed and one started, both being on the north wall.

The construction is visible as the photographer faces north, looking toward the Monongahela River. As the walls were being set in the ground, there were artifacts being found and cataloged as the reconstruction progressed.

As with any large community project, there were many descendants of the early area families who waited anxiously and with pride for the completion of the project. This is a photograph of the first permanent Prickett's Fort State Park sign, erected in 1976.

Shown here is an aerial view of the fort and the progress being made on the fort's reconstruction. The fort is 110 square feet, and its walls are 12 feet high. It has four corner blockhouses, 16 small cabins, and two large central buildings. About 85 percent of the fort reconstruction had been completed at the time of this photograph.

This is a view of a half-finished fort with construction material lying about. Note the two tourists walking around looking at the progress. This was an uncommon sight for a community to have a fort being constructed in their own backyard. Also note the absence of caution tape and security fences, which would be common and required at a construction site today.

This photograph is a view of one of the blockhouses, looking up through an unfinished cabin roof. One record that does not exist is the countless man-hours that went into the reconstruction of Pricketts Fort. To complete this project today would cost a price tag in the millions of dollars.

As with any reconstructed fort that is made of wood, there are continual maintenance issues, and Pricketts Fort is no exception. Shown here is Jessie Stewart working on the second set of walls, 15 years after the first in 1976. The log walls of Pricketts Fort are set five feet underground and tend to rot at ground level.

Two views of the interior and exterior of Pricketts Fort as a visitor would see it today with well-groomed lawns and sidewalks for the visitor's convenience are seen here. This is a stark contrast to the dirt, mud, tall grass, and weeds that one would see in 1976.

Maintenance work continues every day at Pricketts Fort. A good example of this is laying shingles on a cabin or—as in this photograph of John Merrifield—laying shingles on one of the four blockhouses.

While most forts did not typically last longer than 20 years, Pricketts Fort Memorial Foundation's reconstructed fort is heading for its 40th birthday. Many maintenance projects have taken place. The years of 2000 and 2001 saw the loss of four cabins due to rot and insects. The photograph shows an unidentified worker laying stone for the second of two large cabins being constructed.

While the fort is open for interpretation to visitors, demonstrations on 18th-century tools and building techniques sometimes take place. Photographed here is Greg Bray discussing proper tool usage and care to an unidentified visitor.

Shown here is the Job Prickett House, which shows what was originally the front side of the house. The interpreter in the photograph is unidentified.

Four

THE REVIVAL OF THE JOB PRICKETT HOUSE

In the first years of the historic section of Pricketts Fort State Park, the foundation primarily focused its resources on the reconstruction of the fort itself. It was always part of the master plan to bring back the 19th-century Job Prickett House to its former glory. This chapter will focus primarily on its rehabilitation from the late 1970s to 1984.

Job Prickett was born in 1819 and was the great-grandson of Jacob Prickett Sr. He was also the son of Richard Prickett and Elizabeth Jolliffe. Job was a subsistence farmer providing for his family. He was twice married and had 11 children.

As a young man, Job was given property by his father and he subsequently traded his original property to his sister Jemimah, who in turn gave him the property on the site of the fort. The property had a log home on it, which may have been one of the cabins from the original fort. Job built his house of brick, which he made himself from clay right on his own property. He started his house around 1858 and moved in sometime in 1861.

The Job Prickett House is in the National Register of Historic Places, as is the reconstructed fort, and it is the only original structure still standing at Pricketts Fort State Park.

Plowing and other field work was done by draft horses and long, back-breaking hours of hard labor to scratch out a living like Job Prickett would have done. Job was a subsistence farmer, providing for his family. The surplus crops would have been taken to market in Fairmont. This photograph was taken sometime after the Job Prickett house had been abandoned.

The Prickett Family Cemetery dates back to the time of the original fort. This is one of the oldest cemeteries in Marion County and is the final resting place for many of the fort's inhabitants. The cemetery is still in use today and is maintained by Prickett descendants.

This photograph of the Job Prickett House dates back to around 1910. The front of the Job Prickett House was built architecturally in the Federal style, with some Greek Revival features. These include the transoms above each doorway and the chimneys, which are flush with the outer walls. Today the house is void of the picket fence and the screen door on the left.

The photograph of the front of the Job Prickett House, seen in the preceding photograph, would have been viewed by visitors coming to Job's home from this road. It is also thought to be the road leading to the original fort. Parts of this road can be seen in other sections of the state park.

Another 1910 photograph shows the back porch and kitchen area. It is said that in this area is where Job's log house stood and that his brick home stood so close that a man could barely walk between the two structures. Today, this is the view most often seen and photographed by visitors.

Around 1920, the railroad came through, laying track and building a service road to maintain the railway. The Pricketts took advantage of this road and slowly abandoned the road leading past the front of the house. This was because of continental flooding of the original road. This service road became part of the state park entrance road in 1970. The railroad bed is to the left of the center of the photograph, and to the far right where the longest trailer sits is about where the fort site is today.

Two views of the back of the Job Prickett House at different periods in time are juxtaposed here. The first photograph was taken around 1930. The roof has been changed from wooden shingles, or shakes, to a tin roof, and in the kitchen they added a cook stove. Note the stovepipe sticking up. The second photograph was taken in the late 1960s or early 1970s; it looks much like it was left when it was abandoned in the late 1950s. Between the failures to maintain the home and vandalism, the house restoration, which began in 1978, was almost made unthinkable.

Work begins on the Job Prickett House, and most of the early work was stabilization of the brick walls and the foundation. The house was excavated around the exterior and several artifacts were recovered during the restoration. The sifting of the excavated dirt went on sporadically through the late 1980s and was finally completed in 1995.

In the 1950s, a concrete porch floor was added to the house. This photograph shows the removal of that concrete to restore the house back to the time the house was moved into, which was 1861. Once again, this is where a log house stood and is believed to be part of the original fort.

This is a view of the southern wall of the Job Prickett House before restoration. The brick that is in the two-story section was actually bulging and was ready to collapse. Many of the bricks used in the restoration of the Job Prickett House came from a sister house, the Jacob Prickett House.

A brick mason is restoring the bulging section of the south wall. As this work was being done, other brick work was to be completed in the way of repointing the brick. Repointing is a time-consuming process of removing a portion of the mortar between each brick and replacing it with new mortar.

Work continues on the bulging section of the wall—note the large pile of stacked bricks in the lower left corner of the photograph. As with the fort construction in the previous chapter, the reader will notice the lack of caution tape. Today in this section of wall, a visitor will notice a slight unevenness in the color of the brick.

This is a photograph of the south wall after restoration. The reader can see the difference in the brick, which was reclaimed brick from some of the other homes of Job Prickett's siblings that had fallen into disrepair.

This photograph shows workers installing the new tin roof. Almost all of the 19th- and 20th-century structures in the park have standing-seam roofs. This is a feature that is very cost effective and low maintenance.

This photograph shows some of the windows and door transoms out for repair and some new glass. The Job Prickett House still retains some of its original glass, which is hard to believe after some of the vandalism the house endured.

This photograph was taken of the Job Prickett House dedication and ribbon-cutting ceremony in 1984. A very large crowd turned out for the ceremony. Standing in the photograph is Irene Prickett who, almost by herself, saved the Job Prickett House from the wrecking ball. Seated from left to right are Cecily Enos, an unidentified woman, and Jack "Hard Rock" Bunner.

This is the interior of the kitchen as it would have been in the 1860s. Just like today, the kitchen was a place to gather and enjoy the family.

This photograph shows a brick mason at work on the south side of the Job Prickett House. The photograph was taken from inside of the house—note the steps leading to the second floor. The mortar was analyzed by Fairmont State University to keep it consistent with the rest of the house.

Workers remove the windows and support the porch roof. Note the backhoe holding up the porch roof while a worker puts in temporary supports. This restoration lasted from 1978 to 1984 as funds became available.

This photograph is the actual ribbon cutting, performed by Irene Prickett. From left to right are Congressman Alan Mollohan, unidentified, Irene Prickett, Sharon Rockefeller, and unidentified.

Irene Prickett is visible here as a young lady in the 1940s. Irene had a strong disposition. She was a well-respected schoolteacher who taught many in the Fairmont community about West Virginia and local history. She was a genealogist, researching her family as well as others, and she was a longtime board member of the Pricketts Fort Memorial Foundation. (Courtesy of Lee and Kimberlee Miller.)

Five

THE FORT TODAY

The purpose of the foundation is to commemorate the people and events of the Prickett Fort community during the first century of the American experience. The foundation seeks to foster an appreciation of the past in anyone from the curious to the scholar. This will be accomplished through the preservation of buildings and artifacts, educational programming and living history interpretation, and entertainment and recreational opportunities.

The mission statement is for the foundation's board of directors and the executive director to use as a guide for all programming within the historic park. The mission statement is the catalyst for the type of programs, school tours, and staffing that the Pricketts Fort Memorial Foundation wishes to execute on a day-to-day basis.

This chapter will show the reader the scope of the interpretation and programming Pricketts Fort offers the visitor on a day-to-day basis and the educational opportunities offered to students from 1976, when the fort first opened, through 40 years of operation into the 21st century.

This gathering inside what is known as the meetinghouse was probably photographed in early May or June 1975. No furnishings from the 18th century are visible, except for the spinning wheel and yarn winder. Today, this building houses most of the tools used in domestic life during the 18th century, including spinning, weaving, and hearth cooking.

A photograph from 1976 shows the inside of the meetinghouse. The man in the photograph, Bill Wilcox, demonstrates a yarn winder or skeiner. Bill Wilcox was an amateur historian, archaeologist, board member, member of the Marion County Historical Society, and a good friend of the author. The woman in the photograph is unidentified. The spinning wheel in the background is 200 years old and is still being used today.

A lot of things happened in the early 1980s. Pricketts Fort Memorial Foundation hired its first full-time, salaried executive director. Dave Elkington became the executive director in 1983 and remained in the position for 15 years. Elkington was very instrumental in securing the funds needed for the restoration of the Job Prickett House and the construction of the outdoor amphitheater.

During the early 1980s, playwright Seseen Francis wrote a play called *Pricketts Fort: An American Frontier Musical.* It ran for two weeks during the summer for 15 years, from 1983 to 1997, and was seen by thousands of people from across the United States.

An early photograph of the Pricketts Fort play is visible here. For the first few years, the play was actually put on inside the historical fort, adding charm and ambience to the play. The photograph shows the large crowds that came out to support the cast and crew. Each morning, after a performance, the bleachers would be taken outside so the fort could go on with business during the day. In 1983, there were 11 shows and 1,984 people attending.

This photograph shows of some of the cast members during a dress rehearsal. In the back is Ronnie Utt, who was the blacksmith for Pricketts Fort for a number of years. From left to right are Larry Spisak, an unidentified child, Steve Haynes (who is currently a board member), and Jim Doyle.

Cast member Steve Haynes played Zaquill Morgan, a true-to-life frontier hero and the founder of Morgantown, West Virginia, the home of the West Virginia University Mountaineers. Jim Doyle played David Morgan, who lived a mile from the fort, across the Monongahela River. Morgan was famous for his battle with two American Indians at the age of 59—a battle that David won.

This photograph shows the small stage area of *Pricketts Fort: A Frontier Musical*. As dusk becomes night, the lights go up as the crowd anticipates the beginning of the play.

It soon became apparent by the late 1980s that the Pricketts Fort play had outgrown its home within the historical fort, and a new outdoor amphitheater was designed and built. Dave Elkington walks the newly excavated ground where the amphitheater is to be constructed. This is just a few yards below the Job Prickett House and was part of Job's farmstead. The amphitheater construction began in 1987.

This is the stage area for the amphitheater. The backdrop for the play, which was being built to replicate the fort and stockade, was semipermanent for several years. This would be the new home for the Pricketts Fort play.

This photograph was taken of the excavated seating area for the new amphitheater. The land has a natural bowl shape to it, which helps in the sound projection from the stage area.

The stage area, the very simple light rigging, and seating area are visible here. Behind the backdrop is the amphitheater building, which has two large dressing rooms and restrooms with showers and a maintenance room. The construction of the amphitheater was completed in 1989.

Dan Weber, pictured here, was the director of *Pricketts Fort: An American Frontier Musical* from 1989 to 1996.

This photograph of some of the cast members of the Pricketts Fort play shows, from left to right, (first row) Steve Haynes as Zack Morgan, Steve Shingleton as the British Authority, and George Fulda as Trapper; (second row, standing) Shauna Maxwell, Candi Jones, Julie Steiner, Kathy Brooks, Amy Knotts, Sharon Turner, Lynn Usary, Jodi Turner, Jade Wilson, Jan Bee, and two unidentified. Seated are Amanda Usary and Mary Beth Fazio.

Pictured here is a brochure from the last production of *Pricketts Fort: An American Frontier Musical* in 1997.

In 2010, the outdoor amphitheater underwent a major renovation with permanent stadium seats being installed and a new aluminum light rigging. New wiring, handrails, and walkways with lights to make it more user friendly were all added. Both photographs show the new renovations, which was funded through grants and generous donations of over $125,000. Today, the amphitheater is used by Fairmont State University's Town and Gown Theater and for free concerts, held throughout the summer.

A local band named Rustic Highway is performing on the stage of the amphitheater. Since the cancellation of the Pricketts Fort play, many bands have performed on Friday nights. Everything from gospel music and polka, to country and big band music has been heard at Pricketts Fort.

This photograph of Nancy Utt, of the group Morgan's Glad, shows her playing the mandolin. Nancy has served on the foundation's board of directors, she has volunteered as an interpreter inside the historical fort and Job Prickett House, and was the interim director in 1998.

When Pricketts Fort opened in 1976, programs like Traditional Music Day were started. Photographed are some unidentified pickers playing inside the fort. Today, music is still played inside the fort during some of the special event programs, with the musicians in period dress of the 1700s.

The two photographs are of fiddle players. The first is an unidentified musician playing during Traditional Music Day, and the other gentleman is a longtime friend of the fort—Earl Woods. If there was one musical instrument at Pricketts Fort in 1774, it would have been a fiddle.

The first visitor center, which was built with funds from the State of West Virginia in 1976, is pictured above. The structure is approximately 65 feet by 40 feet and housed the offices, museum, and gift shop until 2006. The building had no restroom or a place to hold meetings.

This 19th-century barn, built of reclaimed materials, was erected to answer the need of a meeting place within the historical park in 1992. This structure was constructed to complement the 19th-century Job Prickett House. The 19th-century-style barn would become the place for dinners, weddings, and other foundation functions like the annual 18th-century Christmas Market.

The barn construction was spearheaded by this man, Judge Larry Starcher, who tirelessly devoted his time to oversee this much-needed project to fruition. He found crews to help with the construction process and most often got them to volunteer their time. He was, and still is, a very influential person in the community. Judge Starcher has been a volunteer, a past foundation board member, and has served on different committees for the foundation.

A photograph of the front of the barn shows it as visitors would see it. In early 2002, the barn underwent a renovation to correct some structural problems and to prepare it for future use as the new Pricketts Fort Visitor Center. This photograph was taken at the beginning of the demolition process.

The photograph is close to the previous view but taken after the new renovations. Those updates would include resetting the logs, a new roof system, new exterior wood siding, doors, and more. This work was done in-house and by volunteer labor. The barn reopened in 2003.

In 2004, a log structure became available to the foundation and plans were made to join it to the right side of the barn. This would house one of the offices and gift shop area. This is part of the barn where the log structure would be joined.

The log structure was to be dismantled and moved to Pricketts Fort. The people in the photograph are Greg Bray and Monika Koon. Bray would have the task of numbering and preparing the building to be dismantled. It was part of a land purchase by the Benedum Airport and housed a National Guard unit after September 11.

The renovations to the barn's interior are ongoing in this photograph. These renovations would be part of phase one of the new visitor center.

These renovations would be short-lived; nine months later, the barn was turned to ashes by one senseless act. John Merrifield and Greg Bray are sifting through the debris.

Both of these photographs show a machine that was brought in order to clear the barn site from a visual reminder of the devastation and aftermath of a senseless act of arson.

Three good things came out of the fire in December 2004. One was the new Bray Blacksmith Shop; the second a brand-new, state-of-the-art visitor center; and the third was the unification and determination of an 18-member board of directors who banded together to see that these two projects were started within six months of the fire. The Pricketts Fort Visitor Center is visible here as it is seen today.

This is the photograph of the Bray Blacksmith Shop, which was built from the logs of the Benedum Airport structure seen on page 94. It is a working blacksmith shop very much like what would have been around at the time of the original fort.

It was decided by the foundation board to build a structure to resemble the barn in many ways, as is visible in this photograph. This was accomplished very well, except for the second story. This building has everything the old visitor center did not. It has plenty of office space, restrooms, a large central meeting room, a gift shop, and the second floor is all museum space.

To cut cost, the two outer wings were built off-site and trucked in to a prepared site. Both wings were lifted off the trucks and put in place in less than a day. The second wing is being positioned as the installation crew looks on. Construction of the new visitor center began in 2005 and was completed in 2006.

After the outer wings were in place, the center of the structure was erected by hand. To add to the speed, a lot of the panels were also built off-site and put together the very next day. All this was under a roof in less than a week. The second day of installation was captured here.

This is a photograph of the back side of the building as a visitor would see it from the Job Prickett House. There was some discussion over the visitor center being two stories, which blocks the view of the Job Prickett House from the park entrance road.

Two views of the structure are visible here. The large porch is a big hit with today's visitors, and the three windows on the upper floor are in the museum and the visitor can view the fort from there, which gives them a different perspective from being inside the fort.

The visitor center project was being worked on simultaneously with the Bray Blacksmith Shop. The stone foundation was completed and was ready when time became available. In the spring, it was time to start setting the logs into place. Some of the logs are being set by volunteers. Photographed here is Steve Haynes on the ground level. The three young boys are part of a learning organization called the Mon Youth Build, which teaches young boys and girls a trade in construction. Junie Mayle, in the straw hat, is on the board of directors.

The volunteers are moving a log the hard way. Many of the projects at the park require the knowledge and use of tools not used in modern construction.

The blacksmith project picked up steam when two local companies donated the use of some much needed equipment. Both photographs on this page show the use of a small crane to set the beams and roof system in place. Lee Miller, John Merrifield, and Greg Bray are visible in the photograph.

The Bray Blacksmith Shop is 52 feet by 18 feet and has room for four forges and other equipment used during the last quarter of the 18th century.

Shown here is part of the dedication ceremony, with Ray Richardson, board president, speaking to the crowd as executive director Melissa May looks on.

The ribbon-cutting and award presentation are being performed by Greg Bray.

An early photograph shows the blacksmith shop inside the fort common. It is not very large, but it is what would have been typical on the western Virginia frontier during the 18th century. Note the iron hardware display in front.

Another early feature of Pricketts Fort was a working gun shop, where period guns were reproduced and sold. Over the years, Pricketts Fort would employ several talented gunsmiths. Bob Guthrie is working on the carving of a rifle he has built.

Ronnie Utt is working in the old blacksmith shop. Utt is also a talented musician, often playing music at the fort with his wife, Nancy, and friends.

Utt is pictured here playing music to a group of schoolchildren.

School tours are a big part of the spring and fall seasons at Pricketts Fort. This photograph is of one of the fort's interpreters, Bradley Omanson, teaching the use of the two-man saw. Fort tours include hands-on elements to teach the basic life skills of the 18th century.

Sometimes large groups or entire schools will tour the fort. In this photograph, Karen Holt speaks to a large group of students as she tries to set the tone and bring the students into the 18th-century western Virginia frontier.

Pricketts Fort has had three executive directors since Dave Elkington, who held the position during 1982–1997. The next would be Richard Brown, from 1998 to 2001; followed by Melissa May, from 2002–2012; and finally Greg Bray from 2012 to the present. This is a photograph of Melissa May, under whose leadership saw the construction of the new visitor center, the Bray Blacksmith Shop, and the major upgrades to the amphitheater.

Greg Bray, the present executive director of the Pricketts Fort Memorial Foundation, is pictured here.

Along with school tours, Pricketts Fort hosts over 18 programs and events throughout the season, not counting free concerts, hands-on classes, and more. This photograph is of the second longest annual program, the School of the Longhunter, which has been in existence for over 20 years. A large group of participants is listening to a lecture inside the fort.

Many of the lectures at the School of the Longhunter involve animals, like in this photograph of Gerry Barker giving a lecture and speaking about pack horses. Other topics have included talks on old breed livestock and hunting and work dogs.

The longest running program at Pricketts Fort is the annual 18th-century Christmas Market. During the market, the fort and Job Prickett House are decorated according to that particular time period. The photograph depicts the very first Christmas Market at Pricketts Fort, which was sponsored by the Junior League of Fairmont.

This photograph is of a group of shoppers at the market looking over items. The early years of the market were held inside the fort. Today, the fort is still used, but shopping occurs inside the newly built visitor center.

Two photographs of the Job Prickett
House show how it would have
been decorated for Christmas in
the 19th century. That time period
utilized a lot more decorations
than in the 18th century, which
were almost nonexistent.

A carved stone face was found only a few miles from Pricketts Fort. This was part of a display during one of Pricketts Fort's programs: Archaeology Day.

Another program, which is a big hit with area schools, is Storytelling Day. During the two-day event, hundreds of schoolchildren come to listen to Appalachian-style folk tales. One of the storytellers from the West Virginia Storytelling Guild is pictured here.

Two photographs of the Jacob Prickett Jr. House, which is about a quarter of a mile west of Pricketts Fort, are seen here. This house was built in 1781, during the time of the fort. It too suffered a devastating fire just two months after the fire of the barn at Pricketts Fort. (Both, courtesy of Lee and Kimberlee Miller.)

Since the community and volunteers are a big part of what Pricketts Fort is about, this photograph of Dixie Yann, who is a board member of the Pricketts Fort Memorial Foundation, is indicative of the spirit of volunteerism. She is pictured helping out during one of Pricketts Fort's school tours.

Volunteerism accounts for hundreds of man-hours a year. Without this help, Pricketts Fort could not begin to execute the type of programming it does throughout the year. From volunteer interpreters, to musicians, to construction labor, and gardeners, Pricketts Fort relies on these people to support its staff. Part of the Mon Youth Build is visible helping with the construction of the Bray Blacksmith Shop.

Native Americans were the reason Pricketts Fort was originally built in 1774. This photograph of an indigenous person's dwelling, known as a wigwam, is part of the historic experience at Pricketts Fort today.

Some reenactors in the early 1970s are walking on the original road. This might have been what it looked like during a time of forting up in the 1770s.

Jess Stewart, a local contractor and friend of Pricketts Fort, is installing the second stockade—or walls of the fort—that went up between 1989 and 1992.

With a state park comes security and law enforcement. This photograph is of one of the first park superintendents, Richard Dale. Others have included E.D. DeWitt, Dave Lombardo, and Kevin Wolfe.

Ronnie Utt talks to students during a school tour of Pricketts Fort. The blacksmith shop is the most popular aspect of a tour of Pricketts Fort, preferred by students and adults alike.

During recent years, with the railroads gone and a push for more recreational opportunities within Marion County and the state of West Virginia, the rail to trail hiking system has taken off in the state. This is a photograph of part of the rail-trail system before improvements were made. This section of trail goes from Pricketts Fort to Morgantown through areas that were much traveled by early ancestors.

Both photographs show kids' games as part of the school tours at Pricketts Fort. The kids look on as Rebecca VanGilder and Judy Minney demonstrate how to play the Game of Graces.

Two views of the Job Prickett House are presented here. The front view of the house is the most interesting architecturally in the author's opinion, but the rear view of what is historically the back of the house is the most photographed.

Two views of a blockhouse at Pricketts Fort are presented here. The photograph at right is taken from the outside of the fort of what is probably the most photographed angle. The inside view below is how the visitor would experience the fort today.

121

These are two views of Pricketts Fort as visitors would see it today. The above photograph of the fort was taken looking at the northwest side of the fort while the view below is the southern side, facing the Monongahela River.

This is called the middle room of the Job Prickett House. This was the day-to-day living area for the Pricketts and was also the sleeping area for Job and his wife.

This is a photograph of the kitchen in the Job Prickett House. It is reputed that Job Prickett would sometimes nap during the afternoons in the kitchen on the small daybed seen here.

This photograph of Lawrence Smith Prickett Sr. was taken at the Jacob Prickett Jr. farm in the mid-1930s. Note the split rail fence on which he is perched. (Courtesy of Lee and Kimberlee Miller.)

This early photograph of several generations of Prickett women was taken beside the Jacob Prickett Jr. House. (Courtesy of Lee and Kimberlee Miller.)

BIBLIOGRAPHY

Boback, John. *Pricketts Fort: A Bastion in the Wilderness*. Fairmont, WV: Pricketts Fort Memorial Foundation, 2005.

Haymond, Henry. *Historical Reference to Pricketts' Fort and Its Defenders with Incidents of Border Warfare in the Monongahela Valley*. Fairmont, WV: Pricketts Fort Memorial Foundation.

Lough, Glenn D. *Now and Long Ago: A History of the Marion County Area*. Morgantown, WV: Morgantown Binding and Printing Co., 1969.

Trach, Elizabeth S. *The Job Prickett House: Reconstructing a Family's Heritage*. Fairmont, WV: Pricketts Fort Memorial Foundation, 1995.

Wilcox, William. *Pricketts Fort: How and Why It Came to Be*. Fairmont, WV: Pricketts Fort Memorial Foundation, 2011.

DISCOVER THOUSANDS OF LOCAL HISTORY BOOKS
FEATURING MILLIONS OF VINTAGE IMAGES

Arcadia Publishing, the leading local history publisher in the United States, is committed to making history accessible and meaningful through publishing books that celebrate and preserve the heritage of America's people and places.

Find more books like this at
www.arcadiapublishing.com

Search for your hometown history, your old stomping grounds, and even your favorite sports team.